SIMPLE
PORTFOLIO
STRATEGIES

PETER CASULA JR.

The First Step Is to Evaluate the Macro–Economic & Market Trends.

(A Key Step Often Overlook and Ignored
by the Average Investor)

To order additional copies of this book, contact:
Xlibris LLC
1-888-795-4274
www.Xlibris.com
Orders@Xlibris.com

Simple Portfolio Strategies

The First Step is to evaluate the Macro – Economic & Market Trends.
(A Key step often overlook and ignored by the average investor)

Macro – Economic
&
Market Trends

Allocation
of
Assets

CASH	COMMODITIES	EQUITIES

FOREX	FUTURES	INCOME

REAL ESTATE

PORTFOLIO

CONSTRUCTION

I decided to base my asset allocation on both global macro – economic and technical analysis with a systematic valuation of market history. This evaluation approach provides the investor with a comprehensive outlook for the global economy and the stock market.
 Just as important to diversify assets in a portfolio, with risk management strategies on which I have developed a few model portfolios that are flexible for all type of investors.

PORTFOLIO

ALLOCATION

METHOD

The ability to foresee and reduce volatility exposure during the trading year is critical to mitigating huge losses in your portfolio. A simple buy and hold strategy is not enough for you to sit there on the sidelines and let the volatility of the economy and the market dictate your plan, you must take action.

When economic and market factors turn positive or negative the ability to have a flexible trading plan gives the investor the potential to achieve gains and protect profits in their portfolio.

THE GOLDILOCKS

ASSET ALLOCATION

STRATEGIES

THE GOLDILOCKS ECONOMY

Definition of the Goldilocks Economy, an economy that is not so hot that it causes inflation and not so cold that it causes a recession. This term is used to describe the U.S. Economy of the mid – to late1990s – it was "not too hot, not too cold, but just right.

Investopedia explains the "Goldilocks Economy"

• Everything in the Goldilocks economy is fine until the three bears (or bear market) come home for their porridge.

• The Goldilocks Asset Allocation Strategy represents three distinct trends that take place in both the economic cycle and market cycle.

• The rules for this strategy are very simple, it's determined by the model portfolio that is closely corresponds to the current economic an market trend. In the following pages I give a list of economic data and market events for each model portfolio, this is not a complete list.

The Hot Porridge Model Portfolio

- Economic Environment:

  - Low/inflation & low deflation

  - Low to moderate interest rates

  - Moderate to strong growth

  - Recession lows

- Market Characteristics:

  - 5 Month Uptrend Rule

  - Risk 50% in April and Go Away

  - Box trading range, sideways market.

- Type of Investor:

  - For the active investor and trader

  - For the 401(k) investor

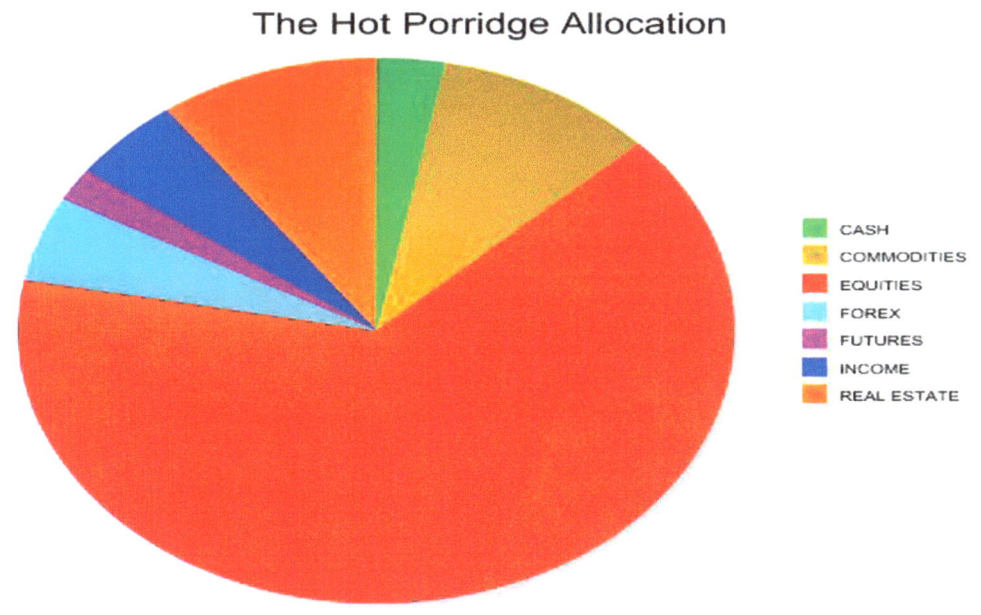

The Hot Porridge Allocation

Legend:
- CASH
- COMMODITIES
- EQUITIES
- FOREX
- FUTURES
- INCOME
- REAL ESTATE

Asset Classes - Large Mid Small & Micro Caps.	Targeted Allocation	Potential Investment Vehicles – ETF's ETN's Individual Stocks
Cash	3.00%	Money Market Fund BIL
Commodities	10.00%	DBA DBB DBC DJP GCC GSG IAU RJA RJI RLY USCI
Equities	65.00%	EWX IWB IWD VBR VOE VT VWO VXF
Forex	2.00%	CYB DBV FXB FXE FXY UUP UND
Futures	2.00%	RALS SDS
Income	5.00%	BND EMLC JNK MUB SHY STPZ TIP TLT
Real Estate	10.00%	RWO RWR RWX VNQ

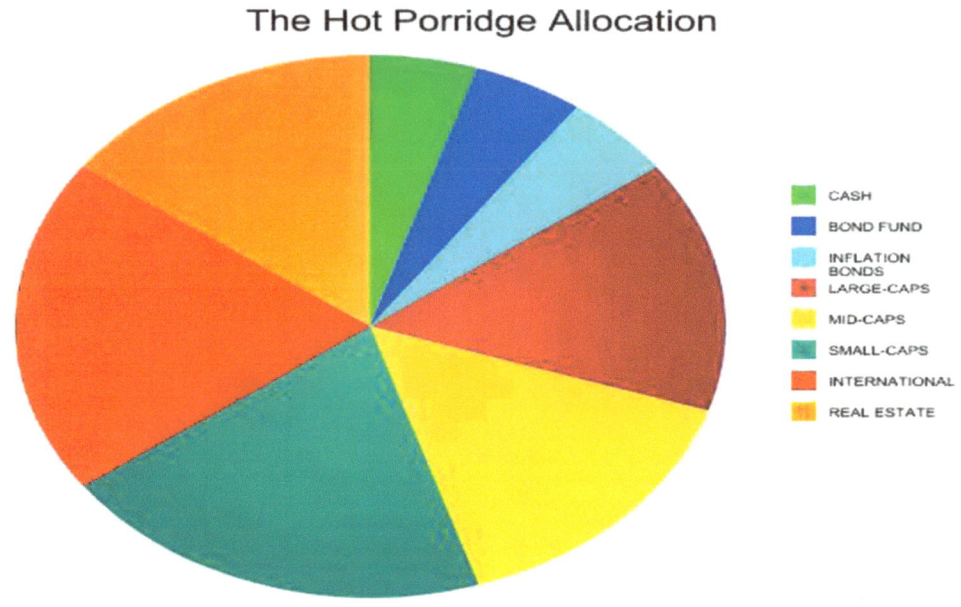

The Hot Porridge Allocation

Legend:
- CASH
- BOND FUND
- INFLATION BONDS
- LARGE-CAPS
- MID-CAPS
- SMALL-CAPS
- INTERNATIONAL
- REAL ESTATE

Asset Classes - Large Mid Small & Micro Caps.	Targeted Allocation	Potential Investment Vehicles – ETF's ETN's Individual Stocks
Cash	5.00%	Money Market or Stable Value Fund
Bond Fund	5.00%	PIMCO Total Return Fund Vanguard Total Bond Market Index Fund
Inflation Bonds	5.00%	Black Rock Inflation Portfolio PIMCO VIT Real Return Portfolio
Large-Caps	15.00%	Large Cap. Value Funds S&P 500 Index Vanguard Index Fund
Mid-Caps	15.00%	Fidelity VIP Mid-Cap. Portfolio Mid Cap. Index Fund
Small-Caps	20.00%	BlackRock Russell 2000 Index Small Cap. Value Fund
International Equity	20.00%	International Equity Funds
Real Estate	15.00%	DFA Real Estate Securities

The Just Right Porridge Model Portfolio

- Economic Environment:

  - Low/Inflation & Low Deflation

  - Low to Moderate Interest Rates

  - Low to Moderate Growth

- Market Characteristics:

  - 5 Month Uptrend Rule

  - Risk 50% in April and Go Away

  - Box trading range

- Type of Investor:

  - For the active investor and trader

  - For the 401(k) investor

The Just Right Porridge Allocation

Legend:
- CASH
- COMMODITIES
- EQUITIES
- FOREX
- FUTURES
- INCOME
- REAL ESTATE

Asset Classes - Large Mid Small & Micro Caps.	Targeted Allocation	Potential Investment Vehicles – ETF's ETN's Individual Stocks
Cash	7.00%	Money Market Funds BIL
Commodities	5.00%	DBA DBC DJP GCC GLD GSG IAU RJA RJI RLY SLV USCI
Equities	38.00%	EWX IWB RWX VBR VEU VOE WMCR
Forex	5.00%	CNY CYB DBV FXB FXE FXF FXY UUP
Futures	5.00%	CSM DXD OFF PBP RALS SDS
Income	30.00%	BND BOND EMLC JNK STPZ TIP TLT
Real Estate	10.00%	GRI RWO RWX

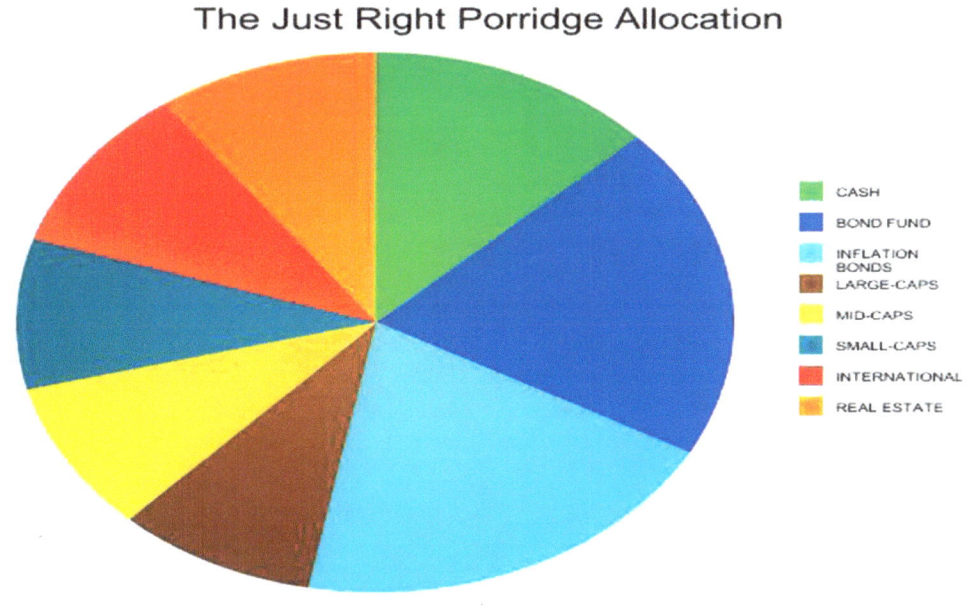

The Just Right Porridge Allocation

Legend:
- CASH
- BOND FUND
- INFLATION BONDS
- LARGE-CAPS
- MID-CAPS
- SMALL-CAPS
- INTERNATIONAL
- REAL ESTATE

Asset Classes - Large Mid Small & Micro Caps.	Targeted Allocation	Potential Investment Vehicles – ETF's ETN's Individual Stocks
Cash	5.00%	Money Market or Stable Value Funds
Bond Fund	5.00%	PIMCO Total Return Fund Vanguard Total Bond Market Index
Inflation Bonds	5.00%	Black Rock Inflation Portfolio PIMCO VIT Real Return Portfolio
Large-Caps.	15.00%	Large-Cap. Value Funds S&P 500 Index Fund Vanguard Index Fund
Mid-Caps.	15.00%	Fidelity VIP Mid-Cap. Portfolio Mid-Cap. Index Fund
Small-Caps.	20.00%	Russell 2000 Index Small-Cap. Value Fund
International Equity	20.00%	International Equity Fund
Real Estate	15.00%	DFA Real Estate Securities

The Cold Porridge Model Portfolio

- Economic Environment:

    - Moderate to Rising Inflation

    - Moderate to Rising Interest Rates

    - Negative Economic Growth (Recession)

- Market Characteristics:

    - Black Swan Events (from the Risk Factors)

    - Market Tops

    - Market Bubbles   (New Industries like the Internet)

    - Party Mentality   (Sub-Prime Mortgage Crises, Irrational Exuberance)

- Type of Investor:

    - For the active investor and trader

    - For the 401(k) investor

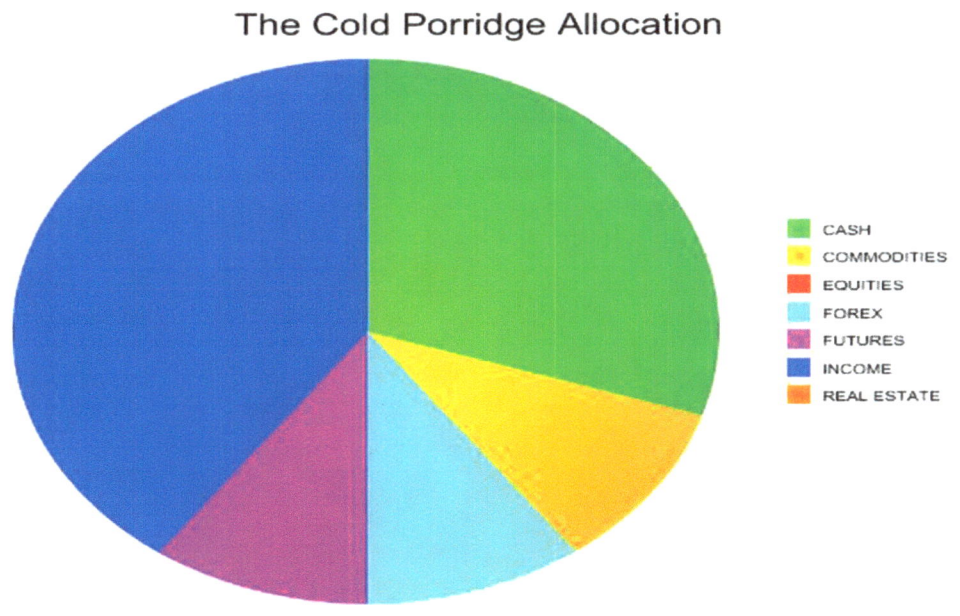

The Cold Porridge Allocation

Legend:
- CASH
- COMMODITIES
- EQUITIES
- FOREX
- FUTURES
- INCOME
- REAL ESTATE

Asset Classes - Large Mid Small & Micro Caps.	Targeted Allocation	Potential Investment Vehicles – ETF's ETN's Individual Stocks
Cash	30.00%	Money Market Funds BIL
Commodities	10.00%	DBA DBC DJP GCC GLD GSG IAU RJA RJI RLY SLV USCI
Equities	0.00%	EWX IWB RWX VBR VEU VOE WMCR
Forex	10.00%	CNY CYB DBV FXB FXE FXF FXY UUP
Futures	10.00%	CSM DXD OFF PBP RALS SDS
Income	40.00%	BND BOND EMLC JNK STPZ TIP TLT
Real Estate	0.00%	GRI RWO RWX

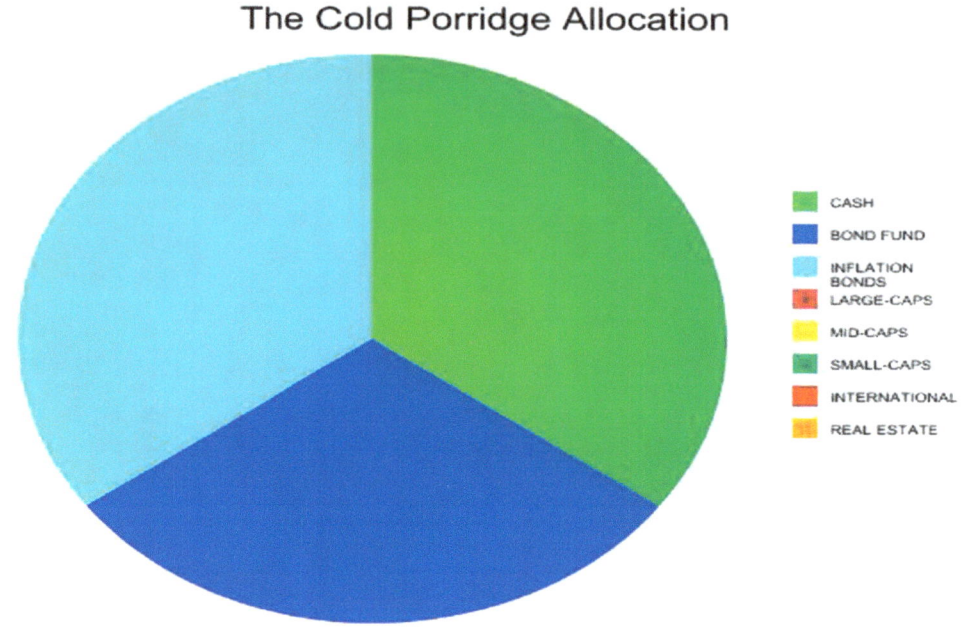

The Cold Porridge Allocation

Legend:
- CASH
- BOND FUND
- INFLATION BONDS
- LARGE-CAPS
- MID-CAPS
- SMALL-CAPS
- INTERNATIONAL
- REAL ESTATE

Asset Classes - Large Mid Small & Micro Caps.	Targeted Allocation	Potential Investment Vehicles – ETF's ETN's Individual Stocks
Cash	60.00%	Money Market or Stable Value Fund
Bond Fund	20.00%	PIMCO Total Return Fund, Vanguard Total Bond Market Index
Inflation Bonds	20.00%	Black Rock Inflation Portfolio, PIMCO VIT Real Return Portfolio
Large-Caps.	0.00%	Large-Cap. Value Funds S&P 500 Index Fund Vanguard Index Fund
Mid-Caps.	0.00%	Fidelity VIP Mid-Cap. Portfolio Mid-Cap. Index Fund
Small-Caps.	0.00%	Russell 2000 Index, Small-Cap. Value Fund
International Equity	0.00%	International Equity Fund
Real Estate	0.00%	DFA Real Estate Securities

Risk 50% in April
&
Go Away!

Investopedia Definition of 'Sell In May And Go Away'

A well-known trading adage that warns investors to sell their stock holdings in May to avoid a seasonal decline in equity markets. The "sell in May and go away" strategy is that an investor who sells his or her stock holdings in May and gets back into the equity market in November—thereby avoiding the typically volatile May-October period—would be much better off than an investor who stays in equities throughout the year.

• Definition of 'Risk 50% in April & Go Away'

You reduce your equity positions by half in your portfolio, you transfer that money into the cash and bond sectors of your portfolio allocation equally.

There are only two limitations to implementing this strategy, such as you'll not be fully invested in the market, another is that market timing and seasonality strategies do not always work out, and the actual results may be very different from the theoretical ones.

This strategy would be ideal for IRA accounts, also there are no transaction cost if you sign up for one of those discount broker deals, like TDAmeritrade that offer free commission trades on ETF's.

- Economic Environment:

    • In all Economic Growth Cycles

- Market Characteristics:

    • In all Market Cycles

- Type of Investor:

    • For the active investor and trader

    • For the 401(k) investor

For Calendar Period April—October

Risk 50% in April & Go Away Allocation

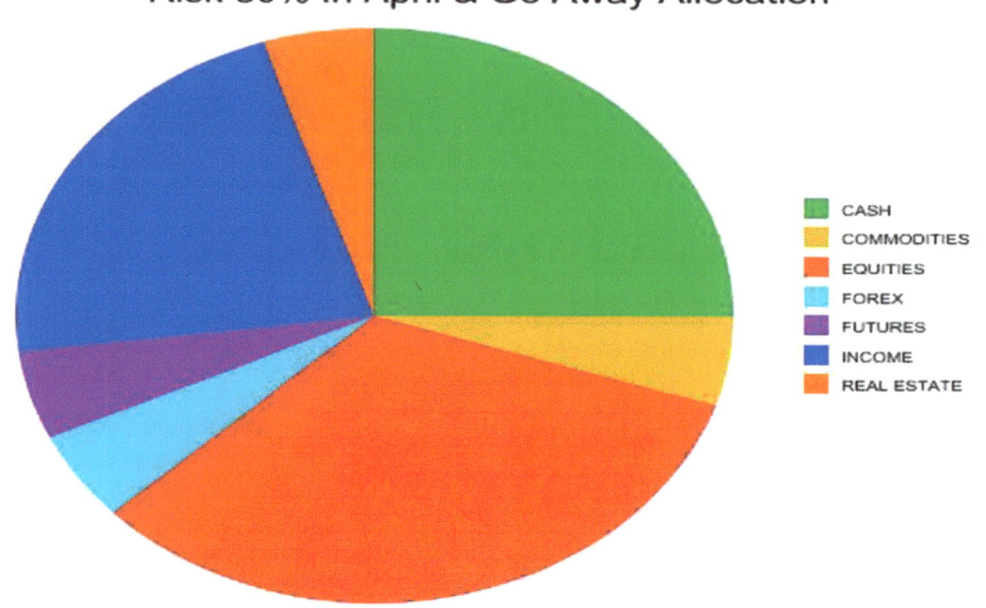

- CASH
- COMMODITIES
- EQUITIES
- FOREX
- FUTURES
- INCOME
- REAL ESTATE

Asset Classes - Large Mid Small & Micro Caps.	Targeted Allocation	Potential Investment Vehicles – ETF's ETN's Individual Stocks
Cash	25.00%	Money Market Fund BIL
Commodities	5.00%	DBA DBC DJP GCC GLD GSG IAU RJA RJI SLV USCI
Equities	33.00%	EWX IWB RWX VBR VEU VOE WMCR
Forex	5.00%	CNY CYB DBV FXB FXE FXF FXY UUP
Futures	5.00%	CSM DXD OFF PBP RALS SDS
Income	22.00%	BND BOND EMLC JNK STPZ TIP TLT
Real Estate	5.00%	GRI RWO RWX

Risk 50% in April & Go Away Allocation

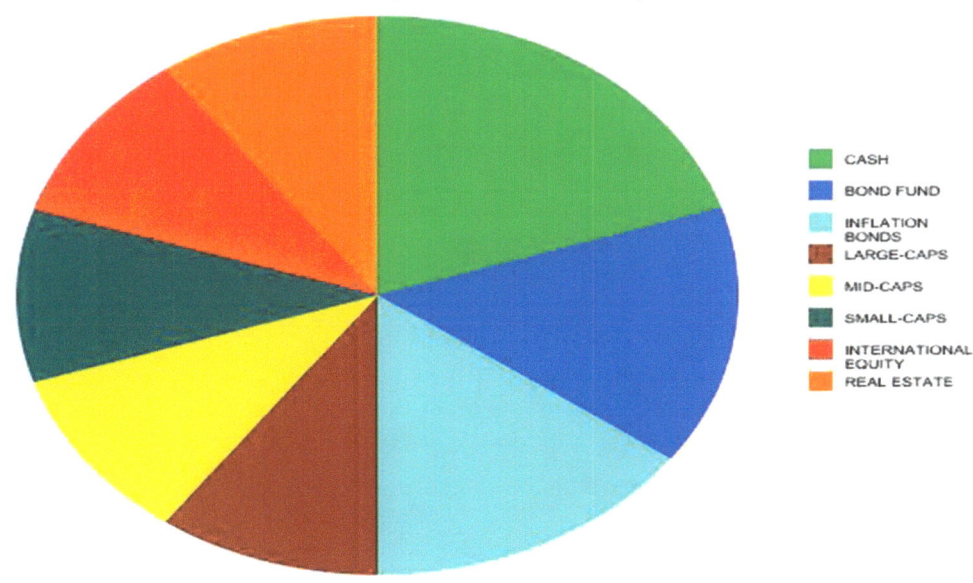

Legend:
- CASH
- BOND FUND
- INFLATION BONDS
- LARGE-CAPS
- MID-CAPS
- SMALL-CAPS
- INTERNATIONAL EQUITY
- REAL ESTATE

Asset Classes - Large Mid Small & Micro Caps.	Targeted Allocation	Potential Investment Vehicles – ETF's ETN's Individual Stocks
Cash	20.00%	Money Market or Stable Value Fund
Bond Fund	15.00%	PIMCO Total Return Fund Vanguard Total Bond Market Index
Inflation Bonds	15.00%	Black Rock Inflation Portfolio PIMCO VIT Real Return Portfolio
Large-Caps.	10.00%	Large-Cap. Value Equity Fund S&P 500 Index Fund Vanguard Index Fund
Mid-Caps.	10.00%	Fidelity VIP Mid-Cap. Portfolio Mid-Cap. Index Fund
Small-Caps.	10.00%	BlackRock Russell 2000 Index Small-Cap. Value Fund
International Equity	10.00%	International Equity Fund
Real Estate	10.00%	DFA Real Estate Securities

For Calendar Period November—March

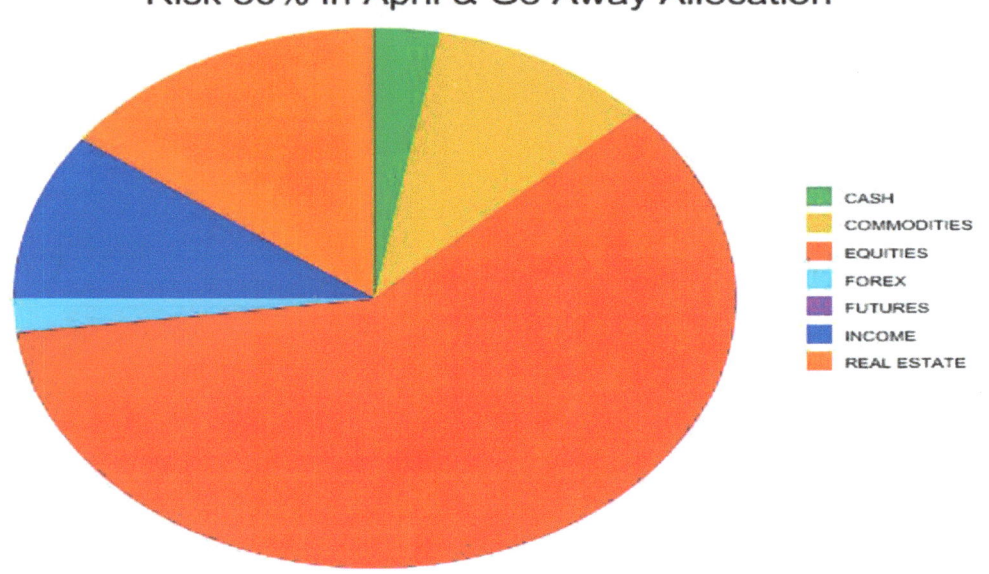

Risk 50% in April & Go Away Allocation

Asset Classes - Large Mid Small & Micro Caps.	Targeted Allocation	Potential Investment Vehicles – ETF's ETN's Individual Stocks
Cash	3.00%	Money Market Funds BIL
Commodities	10.00%	DBA DBC DJP GCC GLD GSG IAU RJA RJI RLY SLV USCI
Equities	58.00%	EWX IWB RWX VBR VEU VOE WMCR
Forex	2.00%	CNY CYB DBV FXB FXE FXF FXY UUP
Futures	2.00%	CSM DXD OFF PBP RALS SDS
Income	10.00%	BND BOND EMLC JNK STPZ TIP TLT
Real Estate	15.00%	GRI RWO RWX

Risk 50% in April and Go Away Allocation

Legend:
- CASH
- BOND FUND
- INFLATION BONDS
- LARGE - CAPS
- MID - CAPS
- SMALL - CAPS
- INTERNATIONAL EQUITY
- REAL ESTATE

Asset Classes - Large Mid Small & Micro Caps.	Targeted Allocation	Potential Investment Vehicles – ETF's ETN's Individual Stocks
Cash	5.00%	Money Market or Stable Value Fund
Bond Fund	10.00%	PIMCO Total Return Fund Vanguard Total Bond Market Index
Inflation Bonds	10.00%	Black Rock Inflation Portfolio PIMCO VIT Real Return Portfolio
Large-Caps.	10.00%	Large-Cap. Value Equity Fund S&P 500 Index Fund Vanguard Index Fund
Mid-Caps.	15.00%	Fidelity VIP Mid-Cap. Portfolio Mid-Cap. Index Fund
Small-Caps.	15.00%	Russell 2000 Index Small-Cap. Value Fund
International Equity	20.00%	International Equity Fund
Real Estate	15.00%	DFA Real Estate Securities

The Investors Income Model Portfolio

This portfolio was build in mind for my Mom, being a Senior, that means taking on risk in the market is not an option.
That said, most of the funds that I've selected are conservative and with low volatility.

- Economic Environment:

  - In all Economic Cycles

- Market Characteristics:

  - In all Market Cycles

- Type of Investor:

  - For the Retirement investor

  - For the Buy & Hold investor

The Investors Income Portfolio Allocation

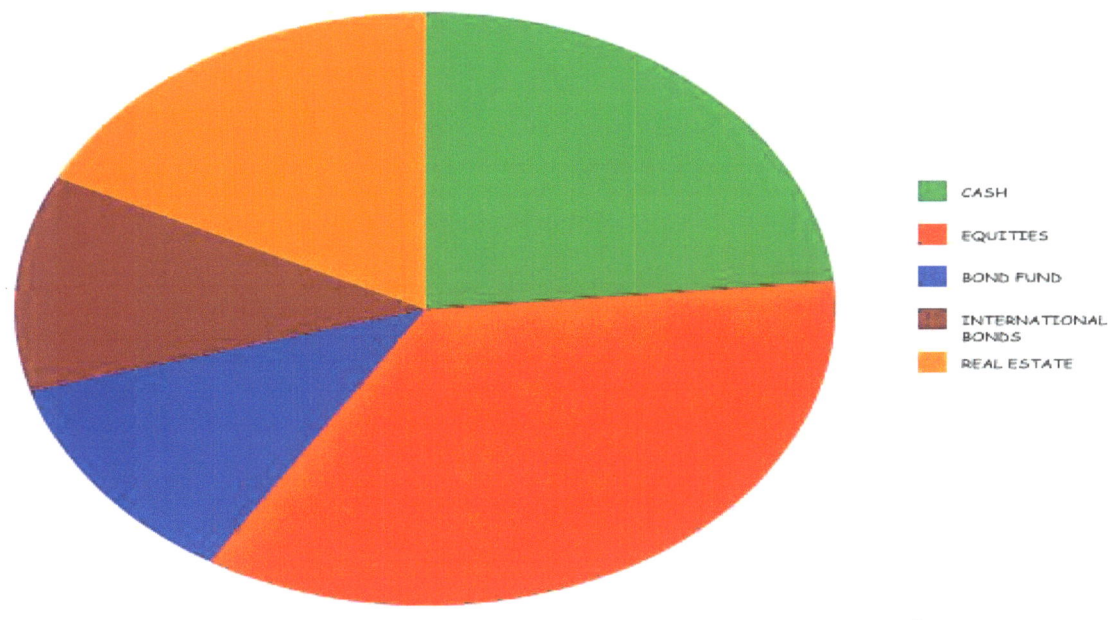

Asset Classes - Large Mid Small & Micro Caps.	Targeted Allocation	Potential Investment Vehicles – ETF's ETN's Individual Stocks
Cash	20.00%	BIL MMF SHY Stable Value Funds
Equities	30.00%	AOK AOM BDCS HDV MLP's SDIV VIG VYM VXF VT
Bond Fund	30.00%	BND CSJ PIMCO Total Return Fund TLT
International Bonds	10.00%	IBND EMCB EMCD EMLC PCY
Real Estate	10.00%	GRI RWO RWX

The Low-Volatility
Model Portfolio

Characteristics:

- ## Investopedia explains 'Volatility'

  In other words volatility refers to the amount of uncertainty or risk about the size of changes in a security's value. A higher volatility means that a security's value can potentially be spread out over a larger range of values.

  This means that the price of the security can change dramatically over a short time period in either direction. A lower volatility means that a security's value does not fluctuate dramatically but changes in value at a steady pace over a period of time.

- Economic Environment:

  - In all Economic Growth Cycles

- Market Characteristics:

  - In all Market Cycles

- Type of Investor:

  - For the active investor and trader

  - For the 401(k) investor

  - For the IRA investor

  - For the Buy & Hold investor.

  - For the Income investor

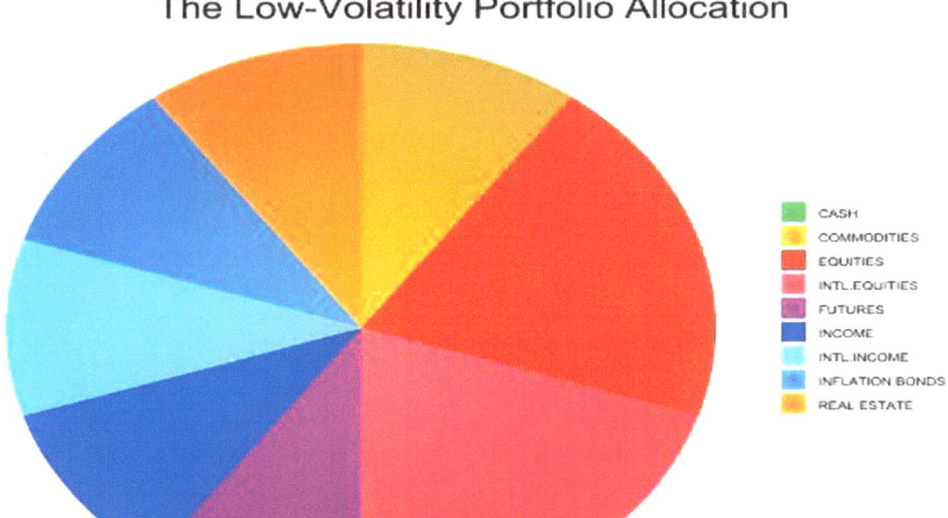

The Low-Volatility Portfolio Allocation

Legend:
- CASH
- COMMODITIES
- EQUITIES
- INTL.EQUITIES
- FUTURES
- INCOME
- INTL.INCOME
- INFLATION BONDS
- REAL ESTATE

Asset Classes - Large Mid Small & Micro Caps.	Targeted Allocation	Potential Investment Vehicles – ETF's ETN's Individual Stocks
Cash	0.00%	Money Market Fund BIL
Commodities	10.00%	DBA DBC DJP GCC GLD GSG IAU RJA RJI SLV USCI
Equities	20.00%	AOK AOM SPLV LVOL SLVY USMV EFAV LGLV SMLV XSLV
Intl.-Equities	20.00%	ACWV EELV EEMS EEMV EFV XLVO
Forex	5.00%	CNY CYB DBV FXB FXE FXF FXY UUP
Futures	5.00%	CSM DXD OFF PBP RALS SDS
Income	10.00%	BND BOND EMLC JNK STPZ TIP TLT
Intl.-Income	10.00%	IBND EMCB EMCD EMLC PCY
Inflation Bonds	10.00%	GTIP ITIP STPZ TIP TIPZ
Real Estate	10.00%	GRI RWO RWX